Treasures From His Word

(Nuggets For Daily Living)

ξ

Tiffany S. Wright

Acknowledgement

I wish to thank the Holy Spirit, whom Christ promised would come as the Comforter to guide us into all truth, for allowing me to again, through Him, publish another piece of heaven on earth.

I give thanks to my pastor, Reverend Valrie Cole, for her obedience to God; as this compilation stemmed from an instruction she gave in one of her sermons.

I am grateful to all the persons who bear me up in prayer; this book is as a result of your prayers as God continues to work in and through my life.

Special thanks to my mom, Gloria Dyer, who continues to support and encourage me.

Thank you, to all who will take the time to read this tidbit of treasures from God's Word.

About the Author

Tiffany Wright is a focused, purpose driven young woman who is passionate about serving the Lord with all her heart. She is Jamaican born and has been a member of the Church of God of Prophecy since 1999. Her guided philosophy is: "For in Him we live, and move, and have our being" (Acts 17:28). She holds a Certificate in Biblical Foundation, a Bachelor of Science Degree in Management Studies (Marketing Major) from The University of the West Indies, and a Master of Science Degree in Marketing and Data Analytics from The Mona School of Business & Management, The University of the West Indies, Mona Campus.

Tiffany is the author of the books "Marketing: A Kingdom Perspective" and "God's Brand Manifested Through Me."

She can be contacted at tiffanywrightcool@gmail.com

Table of Contents

Introduction

This pocketbook of "Treasures From His Word" came out of an instruction my pastor gave to our congregation: that we were to be intentional about digesting the Word of God. She encouraged us to write out scriptures on flash cards and take them with us so that once we get an opportunity to, we would feed on God's Word.

This is my personal compilation stemming from that directive as well as God's promises that have helped me along my journey over the years. I am sharing with you my diary of scriptures.

It is my prayer that you too will be blessed and encouraged as I have been.

Ephesians 1:2-12 (KJV) - Grace be to you, and peace, from God our Father, and from the Lord Jesus Christ. Blessed be the God and Father of our Lord Jesus Christ, who hath blessed us with all spiritual blessings in heavenly places in Christ: According as he hath chosen us in him before the foundation of the world, that we should be holy and without blame before him in love:

Having predestinated us unto the adoption of children by Jesus Christ to himself, according to the good pleasure of his will, to the praise of the glory of his grace, wherein he hath made us accepted in the beloved. In whom we have redemption through his blood, the forgiveness of sins, according to the riches of his grace; Wherein he hath abounded toward us in all wisdom and prudence; Having made known unto us the mystery of his will, according to his good pleasure which he hath purposed in himself: That in the dispensation of the fulness of times he might gather together in one all things in Christ, both which are in heaven, and which are on earth; even in him: In whom also we have obtained an inheritance, being predestinated according to the purpose of him who worketh all things after the counsel of his own will: That we should be to the praise of his glory, who first trusted in Christ.

Amen.

Isaiah 40:31 (AMP) - But those who wait for the Lord [who expect, look for, and hope in Him] Will gain new strength and renew their power; They will lift up their wings [and rise up close to God] like eagles [rising toward the sun]; They will run and not become weary, they will walk and not grow tired.

From My Heart

So, you have been waiting? Wait a little more…

Prayer

Father, I sometimes get weary in waiting. I sometimes get discouraged. I sometimes feel down. I ask for Your strength today to continue to WAIT.

Affirmation

I will continue to wait on the Lord as He gives me the strength and courage to wait.

Personal Entry

____

____

Psalm 27:14 (AMPC) - Wait and hope for and expect the Lord; be brave and of good courage and let your heart be stout and enduring. Yes, wait for and hope for and expect the Lord.

From My Heart

While you wait, wait in a state of hope and expectancy. Do what is necessary in the meantime so that when whatever you are waiting on comes, it fits perfectly.

Prayer

Father, thank You for giving me a hope and an expectation in You, knowing that while I wait, You provide me with the courage to do so.

Affirmation

Today, I choose to wait with hope in the Lord and in expectancy of Him coming through.

Personal Entry

____

____

Joshua 1:9 (AMP) - Have I not commanded you? Be strong and courageous! Do not be terrified or dismayed (intimidated), for the Lord your God is with you wherever you go.

From My Heart

I am encouraged; God is with me wherever I go. He undergirds me daily, reminding me to be strong and of a good courage.

Prayer

Father, thank You for Your presence in my life.

Affirmation

My God is with me wherever I go.

Personal Entry

____

____

____

____

Psalm 3:3 (KJV) - But thou, O Lord, art a shield for me; my glory, and the lifter up of mine head.

From My Heart

This verse right here has helped me through some tough times! Times when I was uncertain and insecure about who I am; times of hurt and betrayal. I pray in meditating on it, that it will also strengthen you.

Prayer

Lord, thank You for being my shield, my glory and the lifter up of my head.

Affirmation

The Lord is a shield for me, my glory and the lifter up of my head.

Personal Entry

____

____

____

Job 23:10 (NLT) - But he knows where I am going. And when he tests me, I will come out as pure as gold.

From My Heart

Focus on the end result: GOLD.

Prayer

Father, help me to stay true to the path You have called me to walk, knowing that at the end of it all, You desire for me to come forth as pure gold.

Affirmation

In all that I face, I am confident that I will come forth as pure gold.

Personal Entry

____

____

____

____

____

Philippians 3:13-14 (KJV) - Brethren, I count not myself to have apprehended: but this one thing I do, forgetting those things which are behind, and reaching forth unto those things which are before, I press toward the mark for the prize of the high calling of God in Christ Jesus.

From My Heart

Look ahead; hope for a brighter future and watch God work all things for your good.

Prayer

Father, grant me the courage to move on, to forgive and to try again.

Affirmation

I will press today.

Personal Entry

____

____

____

2 Timothy 1:7 (KJV) - For God hath not given us the spirit of fear; but of power, and of love, and of a sound mind.

From My Heart

Sometimes I get fearful, but I am grateful that does not have to be my permanent disposition.

Prayer

I release the spirit of fear from my life, and I receive instead power, love, and a sound mind, in Jesus' name. Amen.

Affirmation

I operate in power love and with a sound mind today.

Personal Entry

____

____

____

____

Philippians 4:13 (AMP) - I can do all things [which He has called me to do] through Him who strengthens and empowers me [to fulfill His purpose—I am self-sufficient in Christ's sufficiency; I am ready for anything and equal to anything through Him who infuses me with inner strength and confident peace.]

From My Heart

Believe. Believe. Believe.

Prayer

Father, help me to truly believe this verse and truth.

Affirmation

I can do all things!

Personal Entry

____

____

____

____

Psalm 37:7 (AMP) - Be still before the Lord; wait patiently for Him and entrust yourself to Him; do not fret (whine, agonize) because of him who prospers in his way, because of the man who carries out wicked schemes.

From My Heart

Wait with patience, not complaining, not agitated but with patience.

Prayer

Father, please help me to wait and to wait patiently.

Affirmation

I will be still and wait on God.

Personal Entry

____

____

____

____

Psalm 37:4-5 (AMPC) - Delight yourself also in the Lord, and He will give you the desires and secret petitions of your heart. Commit your way to the Lord [roll and repose each care of your load on Him]; trust (lean on, rely on, and be confident) also in Him and He will bring it to pass.

From My Heart

Stay the course. Continue to delight yourself in Him. Trust His timing. It will come to pass.

Prayer

Father, thank You for this beautiful promise. I believe Your Word and I claim it now, in the name of Jesus. Amen.

Affirmation

I believe God's Word. That which I have committed to Him will come to pass.

Personal Entry

Romans 8:1-39 (AMPC) - Therefore, [there is] now no condemnation (no adjudging guilty of wrong) for those who are in Christ Jesus, who live [and] walk not after the dictates of the flesh, but after the dictates of the Spirit. For the law of the Spirit of life [which is] in Christ Jesus [the law of our new being] has freed me from the law of sin and of death. For God has done what the Law could not do, [its power] being weakened by the flesh [the entire nature of man without the Holy Spirit]. Sending His own Son in the guise of sinful flesh and as an offering for sin, [God] condemned sin in the flesh [subdued, overcame, deprived it of its power over all who accept that sacrifice], so that the righteous and just requirement of the Law might be fully met in us who live and move not in the ways of the flesh but in the ways of the Spirit [our lives governed not by the standards and according to the dictates of the flesh, but controlled by the Holy Spirit]. For those who are according to the flesh and are controlled by its unholy desires set their minds on and pursue those things which gratify the flesh, but those who are according to the Spirit and are controlled by the desires of the Spirit set their minds on and seek those things which gratify the [Holy] Spirit. Now the mind of the flesh [which is sense and reason without the Holy Spirit] is death [death that comprises all the miseries arising from sin, both here and hereafter]. But the mind of the [Holy] Spirit is life and [soul] peace [both now and forever].

[That is] because the mind of the flesh [with its carnal thoughts and purposes] is hostile to God, for it does not submit itself to God's Law; indeed it cannot. So then those who are living the life of the flesh [catering to the appetites and impulses of their carnal nature] cannot please or satisfy God, or be acceptable to Him. But you are not living the life of the flesh, you are living the life of the Spirit, if the [Holy] Spirit of God [really] dwells within you [directs and controls you]. But if anyone does not possess the [Holy] Spirit of Christ, he is none of His [he does not belong to Christ, is not truly a child of God]. But if Christ lives in you, [then although] your [natural] body is dead by reason of sin and guilt, the spirit is alive because of [the] righteousness [that He imputes to you]. And if the Spirit of Him Who raised up Jesus from the dead dwells in you, [then] He Who raised up Christ Jesus from the dead will also restore to life your mortal (short-lived, perishable) bodies through His Spirit Who dwells in you. So then, brethren, we are debtors, but not to the flesh [we are not obligated to our carnal nature], to live [a life ruled by the standards set up by the dictates] of the flesh. For if you live according to [the dictates of] the flesh, you will surely die. But if through the power of the [Holy] Spirit you are [habitually] putting to death (making extinct, deadening) the [evil] deeds prompted by the body, you shall [really and genuinely] live forever. For all who are led by the Spirit of God are sons of God. For [the Spirit which] you have now received [is] not a spirit of slavery to put you once more in bondage to fear, but you have *received the Spirit of adoption [the Spirit producing sonship] in [the bliss of] which we cry, Abba (Father)! Father! The Spirit Himself [thus] testifies together with our own spirit, [assuring us] that we are children of God. And if we are [His] children, then we are [His] heirs also: heirs of God and fellow heirs with Christ [sharing His inheritance with Him]; only we must share His suffering if we are to share His glory. [But what of that?] For I consider that the sufferings of this present time (this present life) are not worth being compared with the glory that is about to be revealed to us and in us and for us and conferred on us! For [even the whole] creation (all nature) waits expectantly and longs earnestly for God's sons to be made known [waits for the revealing, the disclosing of their sonship]. For the creation (nature) was subjected to frailty (to futility, condemned to frustration), not because of some intentional fault on its part, but by the will of Him Who so subjected it—[yet] with the hope that nature (creation) itself will be set free from its bondage to decay and corruption [and gain an entrance] into the glorious freedom of God's children. We know that the whole creation [of irrational creatures] has been moaning together in the pains of labor until now. And not only the creation, but we ourselves too, who have and enjoy the firstfruits of the [Holy] Spirit [a foretaste of the blissful things to come] groan inwardly as we wait for the redemption of our bodies [from sensuality and the grave, which will reveal] our adoption (our manifestation as God's sons). For in [this] hope we were saved. But hope [the object of] which is seen is not hope. For how can one hope for what he already sees? But if we hope for what is still unseen by us, we wait for it with patience and composure. So too the [Holy] Spirit comes to our aid and bears us up in our weakness; for we do not know what prayer to offer nor how to offer it worthily as we ought, but the Spirit Himself goes to meet our supplication and pleads in our behalf with unspeakable yearnings and groanings too deep for utterance. And He Who searches the hearts of men knows what is in the mind of the [Holy] Spirit [what His intent is], because the Spirit intercedes and pleads [before God] in behalf of the saints according to and in harmony with God's will. We are assured and know that [God being a partner in their labor] all things work together and are [fitting into a plan] for good to and for those who love God and are called according to [His] design and purpose. For those whom He foreknew [of whom He was aware and loved beforehand], He also destined from the beginning [foreordaining them] to be molded into the image of His Son [and share inwardly His likeness], that He might become the firstborn among many brethren. And those whom He thus foreordained, He also called; and those whom He called, He also justified (acquitted, made righteous, putting them into right standing with Himself). And those whom He justified, He also glorified [raising them to a heavenly dignity and condition or state of being]. What then shall we say to [all] this? If God is for us, who [can be] against us?*

[Who can be our foe, if God is on our side?] He who did not withhold or spare [even] His own Son but gave Him up for us all, will He not also with Him freely and graciously give us all [other] things? Who shall bring any charge against God's elect [when it is] God Who justifies [that is, Who puts us in right relation to Himself? Who shall come forward and accuse or impeach those whom God has chosen? Will God, Who acquits us?] Who is there to condemn [us]? Will Christ Jesus (the Messiah), Who died, or rather Who was raised from the dead, Who is at the right hand of God actually pleading as He intercedes for us? Who shall ever separate us from Christ's love? Shall suffering and affliction and tribulation? Or calamity and distress? Or persecution or hunger or destitution or peril or sword? Even as it is written, For Thy sake we are put to death all the day long; we are regarded and counted as sheep for the slaughter. Yet amid all these things we are more than conquerors and gain a surpassing victory through Him Who loved us. For I am persuaded beyond doubt (am sure) that neither death nor life, nor angels nor principalities, nor things [n]impending and threatening nor things to come, nor powers, nor height nor depth, nor anything else in all creation will be able to separate us from the love of God which is in Christ Jesus our Lord.

From My Heart

This chapter is worth reading every day! It is such a rich passage of scripture, filled with amazing insights and promises.

Prayer

Father, thank You for the assurance that comes through the power of this scripture. May all who take the time to read and meditate on it receive the depth of revelation that lies therein.

Affirmation

I affirm the truths in this chapter in my life today. Amen.

Personal Entry

____

____

____

____

____

____

Philippians 4:6-7 (AMP) - Do not be anxious or worried about anything, but in everything [every circumstance and situation] by prayer and petition with thanksgiving, continue to make your [specific] requests known to God. 7 And the peace of God [that peace which reassures the heart, that peace] which transcends all understanding, [that peace which] stands guard over your hearts and your minds in Christ Jesus [is yours].

From My Heart

Sometimes I get anxious. I am, however, grateful for this verse that tells me not to get anxious and it doesn't leave me hanging; it further tells me what to do instead.

Prayer

Father, I thank You that when I talk to You about everything and make my petitions to You, with thanksgiving, that You give me Your peace.

Affirmation

I will be anxious for nothing, but I will put everything (be specific) to the Lord in prayer, not forgetting to give thanks.

Personal Entry

____

____

____

____

____

____

____

____

____

____

Matthew 7:8 (AMPC) - For everyone who keeps on asking receives; and he who keeps on seeking finds; and to him who keeps on knocking, [the door] will be opened.

From My Heart

Never stop asking, seeking, or knocking!

Prayer

Father, thank You that You never get tired of me asking, seeking, or knocking.

Affirmation

I will ask. I will seek. I will knock.

Personal Entry

____

____

____

____

____

Jeremiah 29:11 (AMP) – 'For I know the plans and thoughts that I have for you,' says the Lord, 'plans for peace and well-being and not for disaster, to give you a future and a hope.'

From My Heart

Wow, what a promise this is! No matter where you are in life, or what is happening, just remember this promise. God's got you!

Prayer

Father, I bless You and I thank You that Your intentions towards me are favorable, to give me a bright future.

Affirmation

It can only get better!

Personal Entry

____

____

____

Romans 15:13 (KJV) - Now the God of hope fill you with all joy and peace in believing, that ye may abound in hope, through the power of the Holy Ghost.

From My Heart

I love this verse. It is a proclamation, one that we can freely receive.

Prayer

God of hope, may You fill me with joy and peace in believing that I may abound in hope through the power of the Holy Ghost. Amen.

Affirmation

I receive God's joy and peace, and I live in hope.

Personal Entry

____

____

____

____

Proverbs 16:3 (AMPC) - Roll your works upon the Lord [commit and trust them wholly to Him; He will cause your thoughts to become agreeable to His will, and] so shall your plans be established and succeed.

From My Heart

Put everything to God. He is able.

Prayer

Abba, I am encouraged by Your Word in this scripture and I place all my desires before You with the expectation and hope that they become agreeable to Your will, and as a result, will be established and be successful.

Affirmation

I will commit all my plans to God; so shall they be established.

Personal Entry

____

____

Isaiah 30:18 (KJV) - And therefore will the LORD wait, that he may be gracious unto you, and therefore will he be exalted, that he may have mercy upon you: for the LORD is a God of judgment: blessed are all they that wait for him.

From My Heart

It can get daunting sometimes when you are waiting for a while, but God brought this verse to me at a time when I was questioning my "waiting." I am so happy that I am called blessed when I choose to wait on Him.

Prayer

Father, grant me the courage, perseverance, and grace to **wait.**

Affirmation

I am blessed when I wait.

Personal Entry

____

____

Proverbs 19:21 (NIV) - Many are the plans in a person's heart, but it is the LORD's purpose that prevails.

From My Heart

I pride myself on setting goals and staying focused. However, none of it matters if it is not in accordance with God's will and purpose.

Prayer

Father, may the things that I desire be the things You desire for me. May our purposes align, Yours and mine, and may we become one, even as You and Jesus are one.

Affirmation

I will plan with His purpose in mind.

Personal Entry

____

____

____

Jeremiah 33:3 (KJV) - Call unto me, and I will answer thee, and show thee great and mighty things, which thou knowest not.

From My Heart

I think I am afraid at times to see scripture fulfill. This one is a case in point. God is daring us; will we take the dare?

Prayer

Father, I thank You that You want me to experience great and mighty things; therefore, I call on You today.

Affirmation

I choose to call unto God and I believe His Word that says He will show me great and mighty things.

Personal Entry

____

____

____

Isaiah 65:24 (KJV) - And it shall come to pass, that before they call, I will answer; and while they are yet speaking, I will hear.

Isaiah 65:24 (NIV) - Before they call I will answer; while they are still speaking I will hear.

From My Heart

It is already done. The answer is already given.

Prayer

Father, I thank You for the manifestation of the answers to my prayers because You have already answered.

Affirmation

I believe that before I call on the Lord, He answers me.

Personal Entry

____

____

____

*Proverbs 3:5-6 (KJV) - Trust in the L*ORD *with all thine heart; and lean not unto thine own understanding. In all thy ways acknowledge him, and he shall direct thy paths. (emphasis mine).*

From My Heart

This is a known scripture, known based on recital but I am not too sure it is known based on experiences. This is a powerful verse, a heavy one, almost as heavy as Jesus praying in the garden of Gethsemane to "let this cup pass, nevertheless, not My will BUT yours be done."

Prayer

Father, help me to trust You with ALL my heart, to not go off my own understanding but to put You at the fore and trust You to direct my paths.

Affirmation

I will trust in the Lord.

Personal Entry

Ephesians 3:20-21 (KJV) - Now unto him that is able to do exceeding abundantly above all that we ask or think, according to the power that worketh in us, unto him be glory in the church by Christ Jesus throughout all ages, world without end. Amen.

From My Heart

Pause for a minute. Tap into your imagination, into the recesses of your heart. What do you desire from God in this moment? Go far, go deep, go wide, go high. God can do far more than that! Hallelujah!

Prayer

Lord, help me to believe the truths in this verse, that whatever I ask or think or imagine that You can do all that and more.

Affirmation

I serve a God who is able!

Personal Entry

Psalm 1:3 (KJV) - And he shall be like a tree planted by the rivers of water, that bringeth forth his fruit in his season; his leaf also shall not wither; and whatsoever he doeth shall prosper.

From My Heart

Everything will happen for you in due season. You are meant to prosper and flourish. Trust God that He has you in the palm of His hands. Sounds cliché, I know, but it is the truth. You must believe.

Prayer

Father, thank You that Your intentions for me are for me to bring forth fruit and to prosper. I thank You for the manifestation of this truth in my life.

Affirmation

Whatsoever I do shall prosper!

Personal Entry

____

____

Psalm 2:8 (KJV) - Ask of me, and I shall give thee the heathen for thine inheritance, and the uttermost parts of the earth for thy possession.

From My Heart

Do we truly believe?

Prayer

Father help us to believe Your Word, all of it.

Affirmation

I will open my mouth and my spirit today, and I will ASK.

Personal Entry

____

____

____

____

____

John 7:38 (KJV) - He that believeth on me, as the scripture hath said, out of his belly shall flow rivers of living water.

From My Heart

Out of me will flow new things.

Prayer

Lord, let the river flow.

Affirmation

Out of my belly will flow rivers of living water.

Personal Entry

____

____

____

____

____

____

Luke 1:37 (KJV) - For with God nothing shall be impossible.

From My Heart

Nothing is impossible for our God. Nothing. Selah (Pause and think).

Prayer

Lord, please help me to believe this scripture for what it is. Amen.

Affirmation

Nothing is impossible to me, as nothing is impossible for my Father.

Personal Entry

____

____

____

____

Lamentations 3:24 (KJV) - The Lord is my portion, saith my soul; therefore will I hope in him.

From My Heart

God is my portion; He is the source of all we could ever need: our all-sufficient One.

Prayer

God, thank You for being my portion.

Affirmation

I will hope in the Lord, all the days of my life.

Personal Entry

____

____

____

____

____

Matthew 16:13-19 (KJV) - When Jesus came into the coasts of Caesarea Philippi, he asked his disciples, saying, Whom do men say that I the Son of man am? And they said, Some say that thou art John the Baptist: some, Elias; and others, Jeremias, or one of the prophets. He saith unto them, But whom say ye that I am? And Simon Peter answered and said, Thou art the Christ, the Son of the living God. And Jesus answered and said unto him, Blessed art thou, Simon Barjona: for flesh and blood hath not revealed it unto thee, but my Father which is in heaven. And I say also unto thee, That thou art Peter, and upon this rock I will build my church; and the gates of hell shall not prevail against it. And I will give unto thee the keys of the kingdom of heaven: and whatsoever thou shalt bind on earth shall be bound in heaven: and whatsoever thou shalt loose on earth shall be loosed in heaven.

From My Heart

It is such a privilege to know the Son of the living God! Peter got the revelation of the Christ and we too got our unique revelation when we accepted Jesus as our Lord and Saviour. He has also given us the keys of the kingdom of heaven; such power in our hands! Let us use that power wisely. For what we bind in the earth, surely will be bound (sealed) in heaven and what we loose on the earth will most definitely be loosed in heaven.

Prayer

Father, thank You for entrusting me the keys of the kingdom of heaven. Thank You for revealing Your Son, Jesus Christ, to me.

Affirmation

I know the Christ; the Son of the living God, and I have the keys of the kingdom of heaven.

Personal Entry

____

____

____

____

____

____

____

Deuteronomy 28:12 (KJV) - The LORD will open to you His good treasure, the heavens, to give the rain to your land in its season, and to bless all the work of your hand. You shall lend to many nations, but you shall not borrow.

From My Heart

Good treasure awaits me.

Prayer

Father, thank You for always looking out for me.

Affirmation

All the work of my hands are blessed.

Personal Entry

____

____

____

____

____

Romans 4:21 (NIV) - Being fully persuaded that God had power to do what he had promised.

From My Heart

Our God is invincible, all powerful, and He can be trusted.

Prayer

Father, You are reliable, and You are able. Thank You for Your sovereignty.

Affirmation

All His promises are sure! Hallelujah!

Personal Entry

____

____

____

____

Psalm 119:105 (KJV) - Thy word is a lamp unto my feet, and a light unto my path.

From My Heart

I love God's Word. It sustains and keeps me, and causes me to triumph. His Word lights my path, literally. There have been dark days and seasons but it is God's Word that brought light to my path and enabled me to see the way.

Prayer

Father, thank You for being the light that lights my path.

Affirmation

God's Word is a lamp to my feet and a light to my path.

Personal Entry

____

____

____

Psalm 23:1 (NIV) - The Lord is my shepherd, I lack nothing.

From My Heart

There is no lack in God.

Prayer

Lord, I thank You that all I desire is in You. There is no need I have that You are unable to fill. You are my Shepherd, and I bless You. Amen.

Affirmation

All I need is in God.

Personal Entry

____

____

____

____

____

Psalm 34:1 (KJV) - I will bless the LORD at all times: his praise shall continually be in my mouth.

From My Heart

Hmmm, it is not easy to bless the Lord when everything seems to be going wrong, but I find that it becomes easier over time and when you are intentional about it.

Prayer

Lord, please help me to learn to bless You in the good times and in the bad times.

Affirmation

I will bless the Lord at all times.

Personal Entry

____

____

____

____

Psalm 103:1 (KJV) - Bless the Lord, O my soul: and all that is within me bless his holy name.

From My Heart

The soul: mind, will and emotions; this is where the struggle often is in praising the Lord. Our bodies will follow the soul. If I will myself to lift my hand, my hand will be lifted. It is therefore imperative that we bless the Lord with our soul. A song writer says, "I command my soul to praise the Lord." We may have to do that at times: command our soul, but all that is within us must bless His holy name.

Prayer

I bless You, Lord, with my entire being, with all that is within me; with my soul. Amen.

Affirmation

I will bless the Lord! All of me: spirit, soul and body.

Personal Entry

Psalm 46:1-2 (KJV) - God is our refuge and strength, a very present help in trouble. Therefore will not we fear, though the earth be removed, and though the mountains be carried into the midst of the sea.

From My Heart

I serve a mighty God. He is omnipresent; that means everywhere and He is a very present help in the time of trouble.

Prayer

No matter what is happening around me, Lord, whether the earth be removed or whether the mountains be cast into the middle of the sea, I will not fear, for You are with me. Thank You for this reminder. Amen.

Affirmation

God is with me and He is very PRESENT.

Personal Entry

Psalm 46:10 (KJV) - Be still, and know that I am God: I will be exalted among the heathen, I will be exalted in the earth.

From My Heart

It is sometimes hard for me to be still, especially because I am naturally a planner and a thinker. I love getting ahead of the game, so to speak, so to be in a wait mode does not come easy for me at all. However, I am learning to trust in Gods' timing and to wait on Him. There is also an opportunity to be gained in waiting, that is, knowing God more.

Prayer

Lord, please help me to be still, to meditate on the fact that You are God.

Affirmation

I will be still and know you are God.

Personal Entry

Psalm 145:1-3 (KJV) - I will extol thee, my God, O king; and I will bless thy name for ever and ever. Every day will I bless thee; and I will praise thy name for ever and ever. Great is the Lord, and greatly to be praised; and his greatness is unsearchable.

From My Heart

My lips will praise Him all day long forever and ever, not only for the rest of my days but into eternity. His greatness is unsearchable; let that sink in for a while. We are unable to search Him all out. We cannot Google Him up and find all we need on Him. His greatness is unattainable, immeasurable, and unfathomable. That is our God.

Prayer

Father, I bask in Your greatness. I am grateful to be called a son and a joint heir with Jesus. Forever and always, I will bless thee.

Affirmation

I will bless the Lord forever and even after that.

Personal Entry

Psalm 146:2 (KJV) - While I live will I praise the LORD: I will sing praises unto my God while I have any being.

From My Heart

The rocks will not cry out for me. While I can praise God in this earthly realm, I will.

Prayer

Father, I give You praise. Amen.

Affirmation

I will praise the Lord with my entire being—all that I am.

Personal Entry

____

____

____

____

____

Psalm 42:1 (NIV) - As the deer pants for streams of water, so my soul pants for you, my God.

From My Heart

There are times that will feel dry during this walk, times when we will feel low and desperate and it is in those times that it becomes necessary to pant for God. If you have not been there, believe me, you will experience it. Rest assured, however, He will come to your rescue, to refresh and rejuvenate you.

Prayer

Father, thank You for quenching my thirst in those dry times when I needed You.

Affirmation

God is well able to quench my thirst.

Personal Entry

____

____

____

Acts 17:28 (KJV) - For in him we live, and move, and have our being; as certain also of your own poets have said, for we are also his offspring.

From My Heart

I am nothing without God. You are nothing without God. Our very existence is in Him.

Prayer

Father, help me always to be mindful that outside of You, I am nothing.

Affirmation

In God I live and move and have my being.

Personal Entry

____

____

____

____

____

Habakkuk 2:2-3 (KJV) - And the LORD answered me, and said, Write the vision, and make it plain upon tables, that he may run that readeth it. For the vision is yet for an appointed time, but at the end it shall speak, and not lie: though it tarry, wait for it; because it will surely come, it will not tarry.

From My Heart

Wow, this scripture! Knowledge truly is power. Through knowledge comes truth and from truth comes revelation by His Spirit. Listen when I tell you, write it all down! If it is just to put it in bullet points or whatever format you choose, just get it down. I am a walking testimony of this scripture and I am still awaiting more of what I have written down to come to pass according to God's will.

Prayer

Father, thank You for carrying out the vision!

Affirmation

I take an active step today in writing down my vision.

Personal Entry

Psalm 90:12 (KJV) - So teach us to number our days, that we may apply our hearts unto wisdom.

From My Heart

I hate wasting a day. I like having a purpose for each day, and even if the purpose for a particular day is to rest, I did not waste the day because I purposed what I would do with it.

Prayer

Father, help us to live consciously, knowing we are allotted a specific time here on the earth. Therefore, help us to apply our hearts to wisdom as we go about our daily lives.

Affirmation

I will be wise with my days.

Personal Entry

____

____

____

Psalm 139:1-24 (NLT)- O Lord, you have examined my heart and know everything about me. You know when I sit down or stand up. You know my thoughts even when I'm far away. You see me when I travel and when I rest at home. You know everything I do. You know what I am going to say even before I say it, Lord. You go before me and follow me. You place your hand of blessing on my head. Such knowledge is too wonderful for me, too great for me to understand! I can never escape from your Spirit! I can never get away from your presence! If I go up to heaven, you are there; if I go down to the grave, you are there. If I ride the wings of the morning, if I dwell by the farthest oceans, even there your hand will guide me, and your strength will support me. I could ask the darkness to hide me and the light around me to become night—but even in darkness I cannot hide from you. To you the night shines as bright as day. Darkness and light are the same to you. You made all the delicate, inner parts of my body and knit me together in my mother's womb. Thank you for making me so wonderfully complex! Your workmanship is marvelous—how well I know it. You watched me as I was being formed in utter seclusion, as I was woven together in the dark of the womb. You saw me before I was born. Every day of my life was recorded in your book. Every moment was laid out before a single day had passed. How precious are your thoughts about me, O God. They cannot be

numbered! I can't even count them; they outnumber the grains of sand! And when I wake up, you are still with me! O God, if only you would destroy the wicked! Get out of my life, you murderers! They blaspheme you; your enemies misuse your name. O Lord, shouldn't I hate those who hate you? Shouldn't I despise those who oppose you? Yes, I hate them with total hatred, for your enemies are my enemies. Search me, O God, and know my heart; test me and know my anxious thoughts. Point out anything in me that offends you, and lead me along the path of everlasting life.

From My Heart

I am reminded of the love God has for me through this passage of scripture. I am affirmed and validated through His Word.

Prayer

Father, help me never to compare myself to anyone. You have intricately created me for Your glory. Help me to be my authentic self. Amen.

Affirmation

I am special. There is no one else like me. I celebrate me today.

Personal Entry

Zechariah 2:8 (KJV) - For thus saith the Lord of hosts; After the glory hath he sent me unto the nations which spoiled you: for he that toucheth you toucheth the apple of his eye.

From My Heart

I love the Lord. He is mad about me. He cares for me. He will fight for me.

Prayer

Father, help me to understand and accept the depth of Your affection towards me.

Affirmation

I am the apple of God's eye.

Personal Entry

____

____

____

____

1 Peter 5:10 (KJV) - But the God of all grace, who hath called us unto his eternal glory by Christ Jesus, after that ye have suffered a while, make you perfect, stablish, strengthen, settle you.

From My Heart

Oh, yes! For those who thought you would not bounce back, thank God for this scripture that reminds us that after the suffering, He will make you stronger and through it, you will be settled as your faith remains resolute in Him.

Prayer

Father, help me to remain hopeful during the times I feel like quitting. Remind me of this scripture that at the end of it all, You will make me perfect.

Affirmation

The situations I face will only last for a time and when I get through them, I will be perfect and settled.

Personal Entry

Isaiah 61:3 (KJV) - To appoint unto them that mourn in Zion, to give unto them beauty for ashes, the oil of joy for mourning, the garment of praise for the spirit of heaviness; that they might be called trees of righteousness, the planting of the LORD, that he might be glorified.

From My Heart

I have been hurt to the ground—to ashes—to a point where I was walking around empty and numb, but thanks to God for His promises in this scripture: beauty for ashes, oil of joy for mourning, the garment of praise for the spirit of heaviness.

Prayer

Father, I pray that for any person who may be reading this who is low in spirit, who needs just a bit of comfort, will draw on the power of this scripture and be blessed by it.

Affirmation

I receive beauty for ashes, joy for mourning and the garment of praise for the spirit of heaviness.

Personal Entry

Isaiah 54:17 (AMPC) - But no weapon that is formed against you shall prosper, and every tongue that shall rise against you in judgment you shall show to be in the wrong. This [peace, righteousness, security, triumph over opposition] is the heritage of the servants of the Lord [those in whom the ideal Servant of the Lord is reproduced]; this is the righteousness or the vindication which they obtain from Me [this is that which I impart to them as their justification], says the Lord.

From My Heart

I love that God's Word does not give us a false sense of reality. Here in this scripture, it is rather clear: weapons will be formed against us. We will see them forming and formed. We will see them being sharpened. We may even see when they are launched against us, BUT they will not prosper.

Prayer

God, thank You for having my back always and for being my Protector.

Affirmation

Absolutely NO weapon that is formed against me shall prosper—not one!

Personal Entry

____

____

____

____

____

____

____

____

____

____

____

Isaiah 43:19 (AMPC) - Behold, I am doing a new thing! Now it springs forth; do you not perceive and know it and will you not give heed to it? I will even make a way in the wilderness and rivers in the desert.

From My Heart

If it is a new beginning you desire, rest assured, God can do just that. Whatever you need of Him, it is in Him. He will make ways just for you. He will create phenomenon unheard of just for you.

Prayer

Father, help us to take the limitations off of You, and ask of You great and mighty things.

Affirmation

God is doing a new thing in my life today. He is not subjected to nature; He can create rivers in the desert. He can do anything!

Personal Entry

Isaiah 41:10 (KJV) - Fear thou not; for I am with thee: be not dismayed; for I am thy God: I will strengthen thee; yea, I will help thee; yea, I will uphold thee with the right hand of my righteousness.

From My Heart

I appreciate this scripture a lot. I am at times gripped with several fears, especially of the future, but here in this scripture, I am reminded that I need not fear, and I should not be dismayed either. Why? He is my God; my future is in His hands anyway, so why fear? God also promises to strengthen me and when I feel like I cannot bear up, He will hold me up with the right hand of His righteousness. Amazing God!

Prayer

Father, thank You for looking out for me in ways I cannot fully comprehend. Amen.

Affirmation

God is by my side today, I will not be dismayed or discouraged or disheartened as He promised to strengthen and to uphold me.

Personal Entry

Isaiah 43:2 (KJV) - When thou passest through the waters, I will be with thee; and through the rivers, they shall not overflow thee: when thou walkest through the fire, thou shalt not be burned; neither shall the flame kindle upon thee.

From My Heart

Through the hardest and roughest times, God is right there in the midst.

Prayer

God, you cause me to triumph and win over and over. I praise You. Amen.

Affirmation

I will not drown in problems; neither will I be burnt in testing.

Personal Entry

____

____

____

2 Chronicles 20:20 (KJV) - And they rose early in the morning, and went forth into the wilderness of Tekoa: and as they went forth, Jehoshaphat stood and said, Hear me, O Judah, and ye inhabitants of Jerusalem; Believe in the LORD your God, so shall ye be established; believe his prophets, so shall ye prosper.

From My Heart

Being obedient is crucial. We can tap into remarkable blessings, if we only trust and obey.

Prayer

Father, help us to be obedient when You speak through Your prophets.

Affirmation

I will obey the prophets of God.

(This book you are reading is in direct obedience to the prophet of God; may it therefore be established and prosper).

Personal Entry

Ephesians 3: 16 (KJV) - That he would grant you, according to the riches of his glory, to be strengthened with might by his Spirit in the inner man.

From My Heart

I am strengthened in my core by the Holy Spirit.

Prayer

Father, thank You for strengthening me on the inside; in my heart, in my spirit by Your Spirit.

Affirmation

I receive God's strength in my inner man today.

Personal Entry

____

____

____

____

____

2 Corinthians 1:20 (KJV) - For all the promises of God in him are yea, and in him Amen, unto the glory of God by us.

From My Heart

It is sometimes hard to take God's Word as it is, especially when things are not working out in our timing. We must remember that God does not operate by our calendar and our days are numbered. This means He knows it all. We must trust Him to fulfill everything He has promised as they are already established in Him and He is in us. Therefore, we already have what was promised but we must wait for the manifestation.

Prayer

Father, please help me to be patient as You manifest Your promises in my life. Amen.

Affirmation

I have all the promises of God as they are in Him and He is in me.

Personal Entry

Numbers 23:19 (KJV) - God is not a man, that he should lie; neither the son of man, that he should repent: hath he said, and shall he not do it? or hath he spoken, and shall he not make it good?

From My Heart

God cannot lie. Let us pray for more grace to trust in Him.

Prayer

Father, please help me to take You at Your Word.

Affirmation

Whatever God has said, He can and will do it.

Personal Entry

____

____

____

____

____

1 Peter 2:9-10 (KJV) - But ye are a chosen generation, a royal priesthood, an holy nation, a peculiar people; that ye should shew forth the praises of him who hath called you out of darkness into his marvellous light; Which in time past were not a people, but are now the people of God: which had not obtained mercy, but now have obtained mercy.

From My Heart

It is so important to know who you are. If that is a struggle for you, this verse should help in clearing that up.

You are:
- Chosen
- Royal
- Holy
- Peculiar (Distinctive)
- Of God

Prayer

Abba Father, please help me to accept who I am in You.

Affirmation

I accept who I am in Christ, in God.

Personal Entry

____

____

____

____

____

____

____

____

____

____

____

Ecclesiastes 3:1 (NKJV) - To everything there is a season, a time for every purpose under heaven.

From My Heart

I love this scripture. It reminds us that nothing lasts forever; at least not in this dimension/realm we are living in presently. Therefore, our seemingly bad days or seasons will change, and this gives us hope for a better and brighter day.

Prayer

Father, help me to trust the various seasons You will take me through, knowing that each season is working out Your perfect purpose in my life. Amen.

Affirmation

I will trust God in every season He takes me through.

Personal Entry

____

____

____

3 John 1:2 (KJV) - Beloved, I wish above all things that thou mayest prosper and be in health, even as thy soul prospereth.

From My Heart

"Beloved, I wish above all things that thou mayest prosper and be in health, even as thy soul prospereth."

Prayer

Father, I pray that for each person reading this right now, that they will prosper and be in health as their souls prosper.

Affirmation

I am a healthy and prosperous person.

Personal Entry

____

____

____

____

2 Peter 1:3 (KJV) - According as his divine power hath given unto us all things that pertain unto life and godliness, through the knowledge of him that hath called us to glory and virtue.

From My Heart

This is such a beautiful reassurance. Everything we need to survive, thrive, and live godly has been given to us.

Prayer

Father, thank You for being so gracious to me.

Affirmation

All I need is in God. I receive of Him today everything I need for life—all things needed to live here on the earth will be provided—and godliness.

Personal Entry

____

____

____

2 Corinthians 4:6-18 (KJV) - For God, who commanded the light to shine out of darkness, hath shined in our hearts, to give the light of the knowledge of the glory of God in the face of Jesus Christ. But we have this treasure in earthen vessels, that the excellency of the power may be of God, and not of us. We are troubled on every side, yet not distressed; we are perplexed, but not in despair; persecuted, but not forsaken; cast down, but not destroyed; always bearing about in the body the dying of the Lord Jesus, that the life also of Jesus might be made manifest in our body. For we which live are always delivered unto death for Jesus' sake, that the life also of Jesus might be made manifest in our mortal flesh. So then death worketh in us, but life in you. We having the same spirit of faith, according as it is written, I believed, and therefore have I spoken; we also believe, and therefore speak; knowing that he which raised up the Lord Jesus shall raise up us also by Jesus, and shall present us with you. For all things are for your sakes, that the abundant grace might through the thanksgiving of many redound to the glory of God. For which cause we faint not; but though our outward man perish, yet the inward man is renewed day by day. For our light affliction, which is but for a moment, worketh for us a far more exceeding and eternal weight of glory; while we look not at the things which are seen, but at the things which are not seen: for the things which are

seen are temporal; but the things which are not seen are eternal.

From My Heart

We are never on the losing end; we are always winning. No matter how defeated we may feel or how dire things may get, it is working out for a more exceeding and eternal weight of glory, as the scripture says. We have the treasure of God's power on the inside of us, and that secures our victory.

Prayer

Father, please help me to keep my perspective clear when I am faced with life's challenges, knowing that the end result is working for my good and it is working to bring You glory.

Affirmation

Things are subjected to change in this temporal realm; therefore, I face challenges with an assurance that "this too will pass."

Personal Entry

1 John 4:19 (KJV) - We love him, because he first loved us.

From My Heart

God first loved me; He chose me, and He died for me. I love Him because He first loved me.

Prayer

Thank You for loving me the way you do, Daddy.

Affirmation

I receive God's love for me freely today.

Personal Entry

____

____

____

____

____

____

St. John 10:10 (KJV) - The thief cometh not, but for to steal, and to kill, and to destroy: I am come that they might have life, and that they might have it more abundantly.

From My Heart

These are the words of Jesus, telling us that His will is for us to have abundant life. The life of the 'much more'; not just a drop in the bucket but life in abundance.

Prayer

Father, thank You for this inheritance of the abundant life. I receive the merits thereof. Amen.

Affirmation

I have the abundant life. I claim it! I walk in it!

Personal Entry

____

____

____

St. John 17:1-26 (KJV) - These words spake Jesus, and lifted up his eyes to heaven, and said, Father, the hour is come; glorify thy Son, that thy Son also may glorify thee: as thou hast given him power over all flesh, that he should give eternal life to as many as thou hast given him. And this is life eternal, that they might know thee the only true God, and Jesus Christ, whom thou hast sent. I have glorified thee on the earth: I have finished the work which thou gavest me to do. And now, O Father, glorify thou me with thine own self with the glory which I had with thee before the world was. I have manifested thy name unto the men which thou gavest me out of the world: thine they were, and thou gavest them me; and they have kept thy word. Now they have known that all things whatsoever thou hast given me are of thee. For I have given unto them the words which thou gavest me; and they have received them, and have known surely that I came out from thee, and they have believed that thou didst send me. I pray for them: I pray not for the world, but for them which thou hast given me; for they are thine. And all mine are thine, and thine are mine; and I am glorified in them. And now I am no more in the world, but these are in the world, and I come to thee. Holy Father, keep through thine own name those whom thou hast given me, that they may be one, as we are. While I was with them in the world, I kept them in thy name: those that thou gavest me I have kept, and none of them is lost,

but the son of perdition; that the scripture might be fulfilled. And now come I to thee; and these things I speak in the world, that they might have my joy fulfilled in themselves. I have given them thy word; and the world hath hated them, because they are not of the world, even as I am not of the world. I pray not that thou shouldest take them out of the world, but that thou shouldest keep them from the evil. They are not of the world, even as I am not of the world. Sanctify them through thy truth: thy word is truth. As thou hast sent me into the world, even so have I also sent them into the world. And for their sakes I sanctify myself, that they also might be sanctified through the truth. Neither pray I for these alone, but for them also which shall believe on me through their word; that they all may be one; as thou, Father, art in me, and I in thee, that they also may be one in us: that the world may believe that thou hast sent me. And the glory which thou gavest me I have given them; that they may be one, even as we are one: I in them, and thou in me, that they may be made perfect in one; and that the world may know that thou hast sent me, and hast loved them, as thou hast loved me. Father, I will that they also, whom thou hast given me, be with me where I am; that they may behold my glory, which thou hast given me: for thou lovedst me before the foundation of the world. O righteous Father, the world hath not known thee: but I have known thee, and these have known that thou hast sent me. And I have declared unto them thy name, and will declare it: that the love *wherewith thou hast loved me may be in them, and I in them.*

From My Heart

Jesus prayed for us! Isn't that just amazing? Jesus took the time to put you and me before God in prayer. He was specific in His requests and it showed us again the love He has for us, the love demonstrated on the cross.

Prayer

Father, I thank You once again for sending Your Son, Jesus, to die for my sins. I thank You that this prayer he prayed was answered and I claim the answered prayer now, in the name of Jesus. Amen.

Affirmation

I am protected from the evil one.
I am sanctified by truth; Your Word is truth, oh God.
I am one with my fellow brothers and sisters, as Jesus
        is one with His Father.
I have Jesus' joy fulfilled in me.

Personal Entry

Conclusion

Romans 10:17 (KJV) - So then faith cometh by hearing and hearing by the word of God.

I encourage you to read these scriptures out loud and in so doing, may your faith be renewed daily and increase exponentially.

My final admonition and prayer for you come from the following scriptures:

Colossians 3: 16 (KJV) - Let the word of Christ dwell in you richly in all wisdom; teaching and admonishing one another in psalms and hymns and spiritual songs, singing with grace in your hearts to the Lord.

Jude 24-25 (KJV) - Now unto him that is able to keep you from falling, and to present you faultless before the presence of his glory with exceeding joy, to the only wise God our Saviour, be glory and majesty, dominion and power, both now and ever. Amen.

Be Blessed!

Personal Entry

www.ingramcontent.com/pod-product-compliance
Lightning Source LLC
Chambersburg PA
CBHW071249150726
48001CB00018B/472